Rolf Heimann's
AMAZING MAZES

2 TWO

DOUBLEDAY CANADA LIMITED

First published by Roland Harvey Studios under the
Periscope Press imprint 1994
Copyright © Rolf Heimann 1995
All rights reserved.

CIP data applied for

Printed and bound in Hong Kong

Published in Canada by
Doubleday Canada Limited,
105 Bond Street, Toronto,
Ontario, M5B 1Y3

Amazing History

This maze on the right can be found on the floor of the cathedral of Chartres in France. Years ago, pilgrims who could not afford the time and money to travel to Jerusalem made their way through the maze on their knees. This was a kind of substitute trip to the Holy Land. When pilgrims could afford to go there by plane, the maze was no longer used, except by children who amused themselves during long church services! These days the maze is usually covered by rows of chairs, so that children will no longer interrupt the church services with their laughter.

Mazes are irresistible to many people, not only when they are bored. Since you are no longer able to walk your way through the Chartres maze, I have redrawn it for you here. So, pilgrim, progress through it and the rest of the book, with my best wishes for a safe and successful journey.

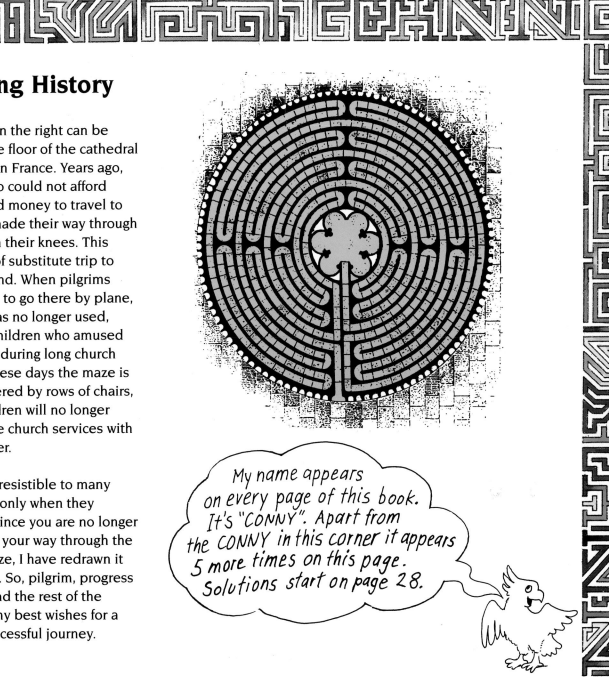

My name appears on every page of this book. It's "CONNY". Apart from the CONNY in this corner it appears 5 more times on this page. Solutions start on page 28.

1 ▷ Half and half

"This maze looks much too difficult for me," said Ben. "Maybe it is," agreed Lila, "so here is a hint for you: turn right 8 times. After that you're on your own. Tom, you go with him. When you reach the top, it's you who has to lead the way back - but not the same way! You have to come back through the other half. And let me tell you - the two halves are not quite the same."
"What are you going to do?" Ben asked Lila.
"I'm going to put up that ladder and search for the three spots which make the left half different from the right half."

Ben will always take the easiest maze, Lila the hardest and Tom the one in between.

5

Only one of the entrances leads to the tower. Can you find it ?

2 Snail trails

There's been a disaster at the International Snail Research Centre! Who would have believed that the snails would be strong enough to break out? There were 3 kinds: the Californian Pink Foot, the Tasmanian Wriggle-tail and the Nanasato Green. Luckily they left their trails behind so that they can be traced. This is the children's job. Lila will try to collect all the Wriggle-tails, Tom the Pinkfoots and Ben the Nanasato Greens.

If those snails keep escaping, I recommend snail insurance!

8

3 Frozen footpaths

"I think the ice is breaking up," said Lila. "We had better get back to the boat. Ben, take the shortest route back, and Tom, you collect our picnic basket. I'm going back ashore to close the door of the Nissen hut. Someone forgot to close it. I'll meet you back on the ship!"

This game is called one-upmanship. Find your way from top to bottom by picking things that are one-up on the next. It is possible that there is more than one way through!

Solution on page 28

Time limit : 30 seconds.

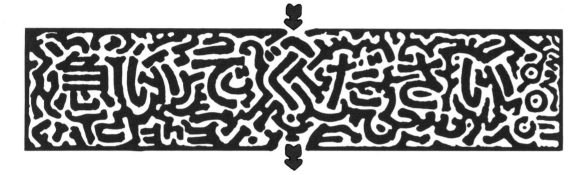

Time limit : 20 seconds.

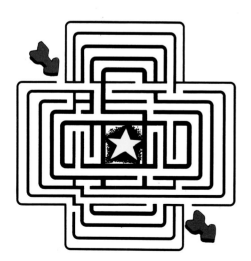

Time limit : 30 seconds.

Time limit : 20 seconds.

Calamitous contraption

Will it work? That depends not only on the specially bred Madagascan Malstock Beast, but on how well the children can operate the contraption. Ben will apply the brakes, but will he have to pull the lever up or down? And which way does Tom turn the wheel to lower the carrot? It is Lila's job to find out whether the vehicle will move backwards or forwards once it is in motion.

I wish they would add a propeller!

Ben, Tom and Lila went to visit their friends in Samoa. Lila will help guide Uncle Tufia's canoe through the coral reefs so that he can deliver his fresh coconuts to the ship. Tom wants to come along too.

"I'm afraid not," said Uncle Tufia. "The boat is already overloaded, but we will give you a lift on the way back. Make your way to the beacon-island, right near the ship and wait for us there."

Meanwhile Ben was fishing with his friends Elisa and Josefa. Can you help Ben work out who has caught the fish?

I hope they checked the tides...

Stepping stones

Make your way from top to bottom by following these rules:

Scissors can cut paper

Paper can wrap stone

Stone can blunt scissors

Water can extinguish fire

Fire can burn paper

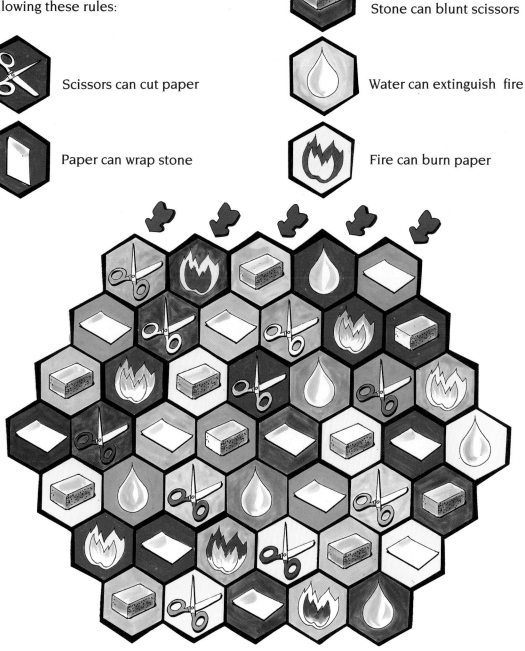

6 Lost property

"I don't know why," said Tom, "but this place gives me the creeps. I'm glad we're out of it."

"Bad news," laughed Lila. "You have to go back because I think you left your cap in there!"

Tom touched his head. "You're right! And it's my favourite red one. But what about you, Lila? It looks like you forgot your white socks. And Ben, haven't you lost one of your shoes? Come on, let's all go back and find the way to our lost property."

I'm not so sure about that. Try it anyway. I'll wait here and watch.

Wait for me! I'll have to look for my name!

If it's true that the letters "CONNY" are hidden on every page...

"I read somewhere that you'll find your way out of any maze by keeping your hand on the wall and walking until you find the exit," said Tom.

"Lets try it. I'll go along the right-hand wall and Ben, you go along the left-hand one. Let's see who'll be out first!"

"That's not fair," said Ben.

"The inside wall is shorter, so you'll be out first!"

7 ▷ Ben's blunder

Ben has built some mazes for his pet rat, but he has made a mistake with one of them: it has no way out at all. He has decided to destroy the maze so that none of his pets are driven to madness. Lila is ready to blow it up, and is waiting for Tom to hoist the flag showing the colour of the faulty maze. Let's hope none of them make a mistake!

Don't you see it's all a mistake!

These kids have watched too much TV!

Colourful connection

Find the odd one out! If you are having trouble, the title of this puzzle might give you a clue. Or is it a red herring?

Solution on page 28

Time limit : 30 seconds.

Time limit : 20 seconds.

What is it that these images have in common?

Solution on page 28

Save the beetle !
Time limit: 20 seconds.

8 Tangled tubes

This waterslide into the hot springs looks like fun! Ben wants to splash into the hot pool, Tom likes the hotter one and Lila would like to try the hottest. Now all they have to do is find their way through the right entrance and up to the correct starting platform.

Conny is not going down those tubes!

HOT

HOTTER

HOTTEST

THE
RICHARD MILHOUSE
MEMORIAL
WATER SLIDE

9 Match and swirl

"I like the look of that maze, but where do we have to go?" asked Tom.
"I think we'll know when we find our matching objects!" said Lila.
"Let's go!"

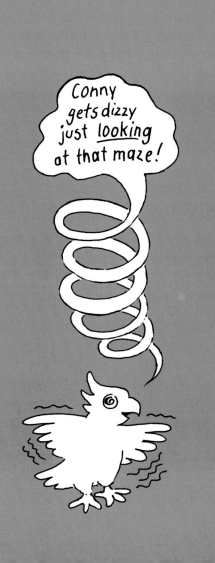

Time limit : 20 seconds.

Make your way to the centre in less than 30 seconds!

**Time limit : 20 seconds.
Good luck!**

You should be able to escape from the centre in all four directions. By the way, the picture is not up the right way. To help you find north, south, east and west, here are the Japanese symbols for each compass point which can be matched to the shapes in the maze:

North   South   East   West

北　南　東　西

Barrel boggle
Which barrel will fill with water?

10   Chow chase

Ben, Tom and Lila want to eat at their favourite restaurant in Bali, the famous Bamboo Palace. However, after the bridge was destroyed in a flood, it's not so easy to find the way. Lila will walk using any path, Tom will go by bicycle, which means that he can use any path except the ones with steps. Ben has decided to go by taxi, and he will show the driver which way to go. Let's hope there are no roadworks blocking the way!

Burung kakaktua hinggap di jendela...

One day I'll find out what they're singing about...

22

11 Parcelled problems

Lila, Tom and Ben have to make some urgent deliveries. Because the narrow lanes are so hard to get through, they find it easier to find a way over the rooftops. Can you help them to find the best way to deliver their parcels to the right owner?

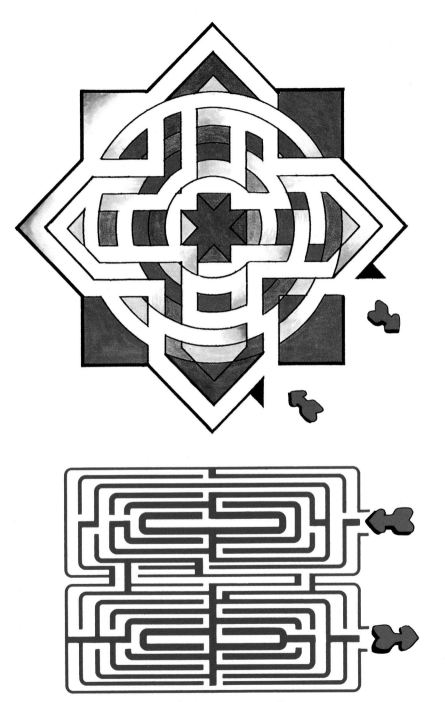

Time limit : 30 seconds.

Three minstrels have come to serenade the beautiful princess. Unfortunately they did not know about the fast-growing lawyer-vine. As dawn arrives they find themselves shackled by the vine's tentacles. The only way to save the minstrels is to chop each plant off at the stem. Ben will save the bongo-drummer, Tom will save the alphorn player and Lila will save the lutist.

NO! Not the fertilizer!

26

Solutions

One-upmanship - page 9

The table has more legs than Conny, but white ants can eat the table, the ant-eater can eat the ants, a centipede has more legs than an ant-eater, but the snake is longer, the elephant is heavier, but the aeroplane can fly, the ship can carry more passengers, but the sailing ship does not need fuel, the house cannot sink, but the skyscraper has more windows, the moon is higher, but the hippopotamus has more letters in its name! The parrot, though, is more colourful, the fish can lay more eggs, but the light-bulb is much brighter, but the hammer can smash the light-bulb, the chest of drawers has more handles, the fire can burn the chest, but the rain can extinguish the fire. The umbrella can keep rain off, a duck doesn't need an umbrella, but a cockatoo can speak better than a duck! Try to find a different way, and don't be afraid to be silly: it's silly anyway to try to be one-up on others!

Colourful connection - page 17

The hat is the odd one out. It is the only item that does not contain the colour red.

Solution to puzzle on page 18

The images have the number 2 in common. Two eyes, two wheels, two birds etc.

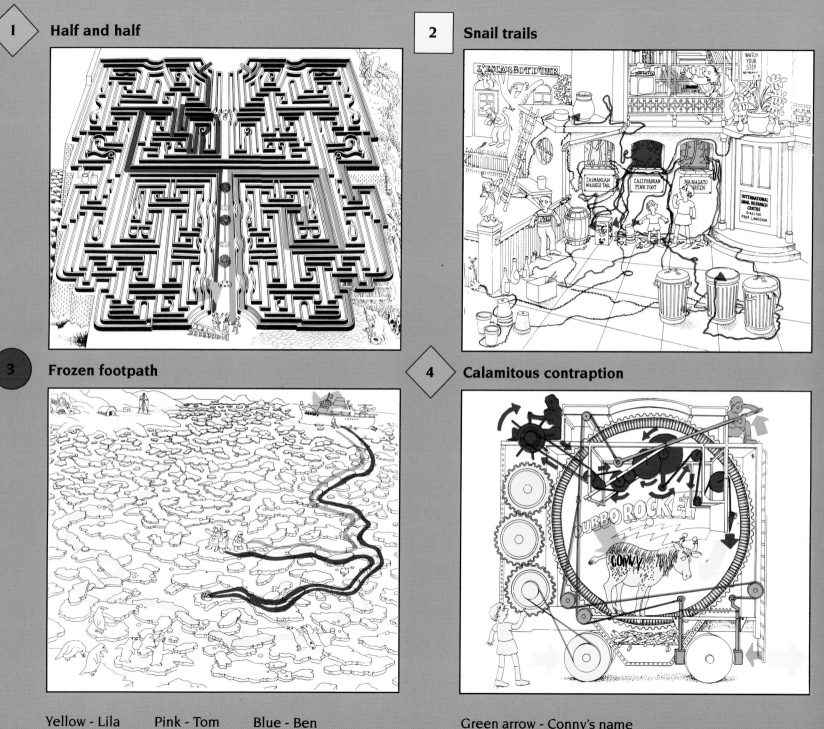

1 Half and half

2 Snail trails

3 Frozen footpath

4 Calamitous contraption

Yellow - Lila   Pink - Tom   Blue - Ben

Green arrow - Conny's name

29

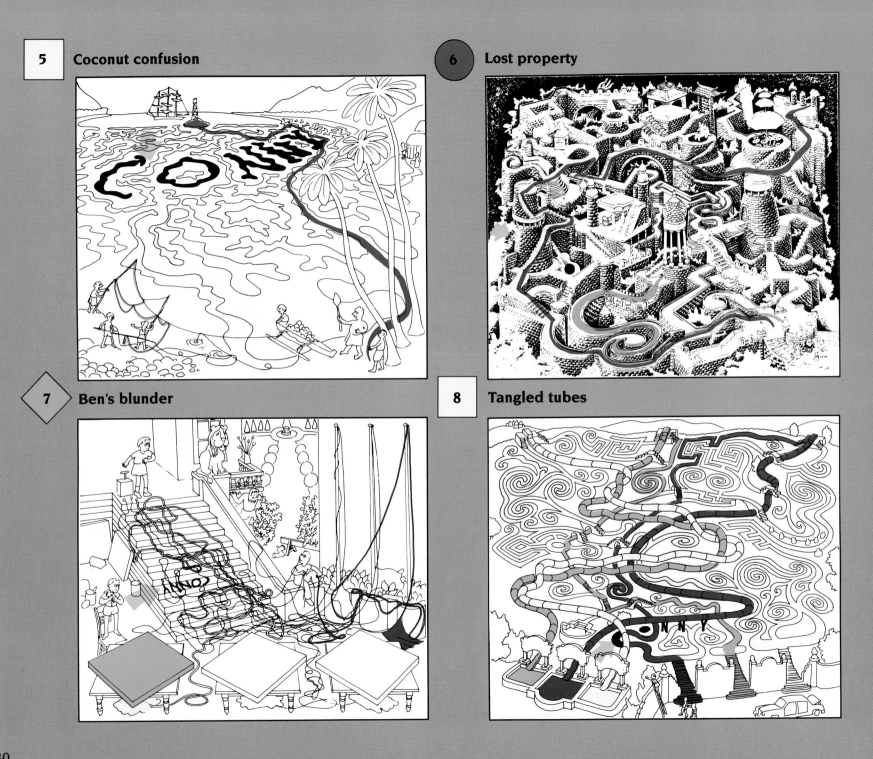

5 Coconut confusion

6 Lost property

7 Ben's blunder

8 Tangled tubes

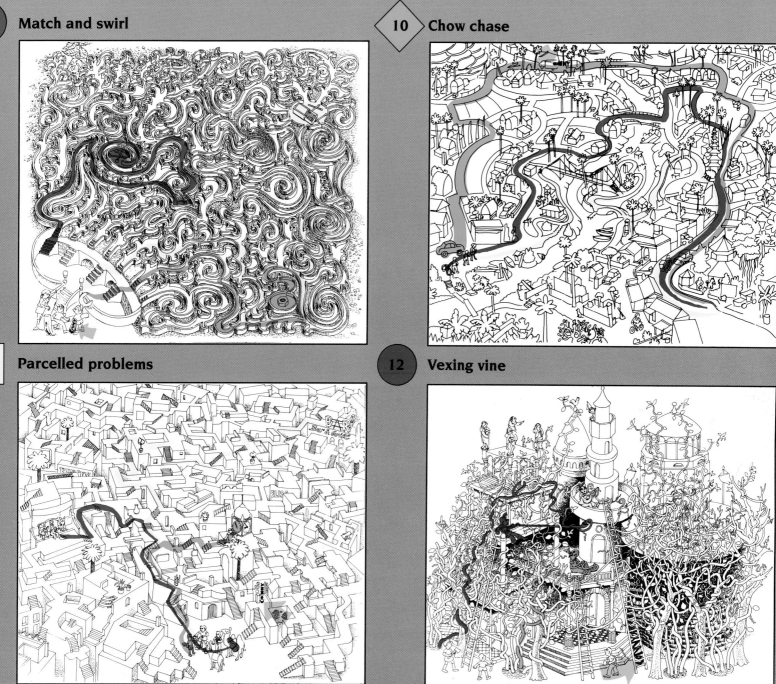

9 Match and swirl

10 Chow chase

11 Parcelled problems

12 Vexing vine

31

"Let's do an amazing experiment," suggested Tom. "Both of us will keep our hands on the left-hand side wall and walk at the same speed until we come out again. When we meet each other, we'll call out and Lila will know we're exactly halfway through."
"Hmm, we'll see," said Lila. "Ready, set, go!"